What Is This Thing Called SEX?

cartoons by women

———————

edited by roz warren

The Crossing Press, Freedom, CA 95019

"Lesbian Bed Death" from Dykes To Watch Out For 1992 Calendar (Firebrand Books/Ithaca, NY 14850). Copyright © 1991 Alison Bechdel. Used by permission of the artist. "Oral Sex" from Dykes to Watch Out For (Firebrand Books/Ithaca, NY/14850) Copyright © 1988 Alison Bechdel. "Spurned for the Moment" from Dykes to Watch Out For: The Sequel" (Firebrand Books/Ithaca, NY14850). Copyright © 1992 Alison Bechdel. Reprinted by permission of the artist. Cartoons by Barbara Brandon from *Where I'm Coming From* by Barbara Brandon. Copyright © 1993 Universal Press Syndicate. Reprinted by permission of Universal Press Syndicate. Cartoons by Jane Caminos from *That's Ms. Bulldyke to You, Charlie!* (Madwoman Press/POB 690, Northboro, MA 01532) Copyright © 1992 by Jane Caminos. Reprinted by permission of Madwoman Press. Cartoons by Jennifer Camper Copyright © Jennifer Camper. Cartoons by Nicole Hollander Copyright © 1993 Nicole Hollander. Reprinted by permission of the artist. Cartoons by Leanne Franson Copyright © 1993 Leanne Franson. All Rights Reserved. Individual panels may be reproduced for review purposes only. For Better or For Worse Cartoons Copyright © 1993 Lynn Johnston Prod., Inc. Reprinted with permission of Universal Press Syndicate. All Rights Reserved. "Sex in the 21st Century" by Marian Henley Copyright © 1988 Marian Henley. Reprinted by permission of the artist. Cartoons by Andrea Natalie Copyright © 1989, 1990, 1991, 1992 by Andrea Natalie. Cartoons by Rina Piccolo copyright © 1993 Rina Piccolo. Reproduction in whole or part without written permission of the artist is prohibited. "Girl's Eye View" by Libby Reid Copyright © 1985 Libby Reid. "Subliminal Message Alert" by Libby Reid Copyright © 1988 Libby Reid.

Library of Congress Cataloging-in-Publication Data

What is this thing called sex? : cartoons by women / edited by Roz
  Warren.
    p.   cm.
    ISBN 0-89594-645-9. -- ISBN 0-89594-631-9 (pbk.)
    1. Wit and humor, Pictorial. 2. Sex--Caricatures and cartoons.
  3. Women cartoonists. I. Warren, Rosalind, 1954- .
NC1763.S5W47 1993
741.5'9'082--dc20
                                                                93-9031
                                                                    CIP

This book is dedicated to my husband Richard,
who is unquestionably better than cake.

cartoonists

Nicole Hollander

they NAMED ME "Sex MACHINE."
you know, After the JAMES Brown
song. Sort of A joke At My
Expense, right? So when I HAVE
to Go to the vet AND SHE Asks
MY NAME, they Lose their nerve...
they tell her: "Frisky." It isn't
ENOUGH I HAVE to Go to the
vet, I HAVE to HAVE AN identity
crisis too?
I could spit.

The Quest for the Holy Grail and Other Anxiety Producing Metaphors

Harold. I'm leaving to look for my "G" spot. Kiss the children goodbye for me.

Nicole Hollander

Maureen Lister and Silvia Valdaura

© MAUREEN LISTER
SILVIA VALDAURA 1992

patrizia de AMbrogio

She says she doesn't like to tell me what she wants because it's not spontaneous and she feels like I'm doing it just to please her, so she doesn't tell me, and I'm not really sure what she likes, and then she says if I really cared for her I would try harder to please her.

Maybe she could just say "warm" or "cold."

machlis

gail machlis

Romance Novelist

I've just spoken with Arthur, and I'm afraid we're going to have to rethink the whole campaign.

gail machlis

Good Reasons Not to Have Sex

But gee, Ann Marie,
I took you to dinner,
AND the movies,
plus, You had
two boxes of
Milk Duds.

gail machlis
© 1990

BY DAY, HE WAS MILD-MANNERED REPORTER BILL CLARK.... BY NIGHT, HE WAS STILL MILD-MANNERED REPORTER BILL CLARK.
R. PICCOLO © '97

VIV QUILLIN

Find something NICE to do

I already have...

"Monica's been on this marvellous self-examination course..."

all on your own-night after night,
what do you DO with yourself Mother?

©Quillin.

The tradgedy of the solar-powered vibrator

Quillin.©

continued...

continued...

Mary Sativa

BRAVE NEW WORLD

BY **MARY SATIVA**

The next day at the office Mary thanked
everyone for the surprise party.

It was the first and last time McClain
and Schwartz would forget to
turn off the intercom.

Andrea Natalie

As usual, Rona's husband wasn't
really listening to her.

Perhaps it was the effect of too much
eggnog, but in the wink of an eye Nancy
and Maura had spilled the beans.

kathryn LeMieux

THE COMPROMISE BETWEEN
'COMFORTABLE' AND 'SEXY'

THE FLANNEL GARTER BELT

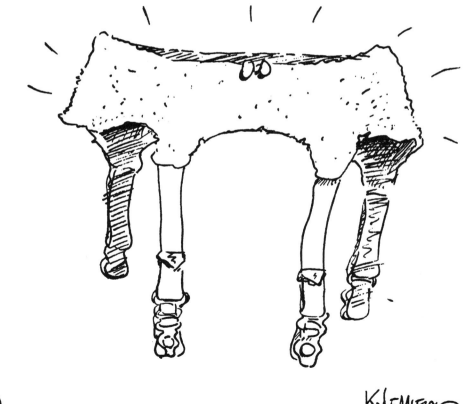

K. LeMieux ©
1992

dildo advocate #2

...it never gets performance anxiety!

©1992 leanne franson

dildo advocate #3

dildo advocate #4

© 1992 leanne franson

MEN: the post-dildo experience

Leanne Franson

continued ➔

Leanne Franson

© 1992 leanne franson

-56-

JoHn took it As a Bad Sign
WHen MaRcy bEgaN smoKiNG
DUring SeX.

ellen forney

Bi Bi BiRDiE!

THE TRIALS & TRIBULATIONS OF A YOUNG BISEXUAL CHICK

BEING Bi is **BOSS**, GIRLFRIENDS-- PERSONALLY, i WOULDN'T HAVE IT ANY OTHER WAY.

IT CAN BE A **TRYING EXPERIENCE** SOMETIMES, THOUGH...

ellen forney ©92

I HAVE TO COME OUT TO **ALL** MY FRIENDS, STRAIGHT **AND** GAY...

HEY BIRDIE! YOU FOUND A **BOYFRIEND** YET?

NOPE. NO GIRLFRIEND, EITHER.

OH! i... OH!

HEY BIRDIE, YOU FOUND A **GIRLFRIEND** YET?

NOPE. NO BOYFRIEND, EITHER.

OH! i... OH!

BUT EVEN THEN, SOME PEOPLE STILL CAN'T **QUITE** COMPREHEND.

YEAH BIRDIE, BUT **REALLY**--- WHICH DO YOU LIKE **MORE**?

☐ STRAIGHT

☐ GAY

NOTHING IN BETWEEN

SEXUAL LABELS ARE **TRICKY**, THOUGH— EVERYONE HAS HER **OWN SET** OF DEFINITIONS.

... WHO AM i TO JUDGE?

CONSIDERS HERSELF **STRAIGHT**.

HAS HAD A STEADY GIRLFRIEND FOR SIX MONTHS.

CONSIDERS HERSELF **LESBIAN**.

DATES MEN ON THE SLY AND HAS A SECRET STASH OF "BLUE BOY" MAGAZINES.

BEING Bi CAN OPEN UP SOME **INTERESTING OPPORTUNITIES.** F'R instance, **CRUISING** ---

... SCOPING **CUTE MEN** WITH **JIM** ...

... SCOPING **CUTE WOMEN** WITH **MATT** ...

... SCOPING **CUTIES** IN **GENERAL** WITH **TINA**.

... AND THEN THERE'S **MIXED - SEX 3 - SOMES** ...

... QUITE FUN.

ANOTHER NOTE ON 3-SOMES --- **LOTS** OF STRAIGHT GUYS GET **EXTREMELY EXCITED** TO MEET **BISEXUAL WOMEN**.

MY THEORY IS THAT THEY HAVE A **GENETICALLY INSTILLED FANTASY** ABOUT **MAKING IT WITH TWO WOMEN.**

DEALING WITH **PARENTAL DISAPPROVAL** IS ALWAYS A **CHALLENGE.**

THE STEREOTYPE OF THE **NON-STOP SEXUALLY ACTIVE BISEXUAL** COULDN'T FIT ME **LESS**, THOUGH ---
... UNFORTUNATELY.

is it REAL? OR is it JUST... PHONEY SEX ♥

ellen forney ©92

ABOUT A YEAR AGO, WHEN i WAS STILL LIVING IN PHILLY, i HAD A RELATIONSHIP WITH THIS GUY ON THE PHONE.

IT'S ME... WHAT ARE YOU WEARING?... YEAH.

OH YEAH?!!

WE'D MET ON A FLIGHT TO MIAMI AND EXCHANGED PHONE NUMBERS.

REALLY? WHAT KIND OF MOTORCYCLE?

AN OLD HARLEY.

HE LIVED IN MINNEAPOLIS.

WE CALLED EACH OTHER ALMOST DAILY. OUR CONVERSATIONS SOON TURNED TO SEX AND ONE THING LED TO ANOTHER...

UH-HUH!?

..AND i SLOWLY SLIDE MY TONGUE UP THE INSIDE OF YOUR LEFT THIGH...

SOMETIMES OUR AFFAIR SEEMED RATHER BIZARRE AND UNREAL...

SO- ARE YOU SEEING ANYONE SPECIAL THESE DAYS?

WELL... NOT EXACTLY...

PHONE BILL

...AND OTHER TIMES IT SEEMED ONLY ALL TOO REAL.

I ONCE DREAMT THAT HE & i GOT MARRIED.

i DO.

IT WAS WAY HOT FOR SEVERAL MONTHS, BUT THEN THE WHOLE THING STARTED TO FALL APART.

YOU'RE SO... EMOTIONALLY DISTANT... i DON'T KNOW...

WELL-- HE WAS ALREADY MARRIED, ANYWAY.

EVEN NEW HABITS DIE HARD, THOUGH --- iT TOOK ME A WHILE TO WEAN MYSELF OFF THE PHONE.

...AND HOME ALONE WILL BE SHOWING AT 7 AND 9:30 PM. PLEASE STAY ON THE LINE AND THIS MESSAGE WILL REPEAT...

end

flash rosenberg

FLASHPOINT   by Flash Rosenberg

I dreamt I was holding my diaphragm up to the light to check for holes. Next thing I knew my diaphragm had turned into a giant planetarium with sparkly dots of light everywhere.

And just like anyone who's ever been in a planetarium, I was wondering, "Where's the Big Dipper?"

chris suddick

IF BARBARA WOODHOUSE WAS A SEX THERAPIST...

©suddick 92

Q. DEAR MRS. WOODHOUSE, HOW DO I CURE MY MAN OF PREMATURE EJACULATION?

A. WHACK HIM ON THE NOSE WITH A ROLLED UP NEWSPAPER

101 USES for A DEAD DIAPHRAGM:

#19.

Elbow
Moisturizing

#37.

Trailer hitch
cover

#52.

Drain Stopper

#94.

Doorknob
Protector

SUZY BECKER

ALISON BECHDEL

MOD-ERN LOVE 23
© 1988 BY ALISON BECHDEL

A FTER DECLARING THEIR MUTUAL **ATTRACTION**, OUR HEROINES RETURN TOGETHER TO MO'S APARTMENT UNDER THE PRETENSE OF **WARMING** HARRIET'S FEET.

H ARRIET HAS JUST REFUSED MORE **TEA**.

UH.. LISTEN, HARRIET.. I HATE TO MAKE **ASSUMPTIONS** ABOUT WHAT'S GOING **ON** HERE... BUT IN THE EVENT THAT YOU AND I, Y'KNOW... AT SOME POINT, SAY, MAYBE GOT **SEXUAL**... HYPOTHETICALLY **SPEAKING**, OF COURSE... AH... I THINK WE SHOULD TALK ABOUT WHERE WE'VE **BEEN** AND ALL, CONSIDERING **AIDS** AND EVERYTHING... Y'KNOW?

HUH! THAT WAS REALLY **BRAVE** OF YOU... I DIDN'T KNOW EXACTLY HOW TO BRING IT UP...

OKAY. SO, I'VE NEVER SLEPT WITH A **MAN**... NEVER DONE **I.V. DRUGS**,.. NEVER HAD A **BLOOD TRANSFUSION**, ... BUT I DID ONCE HAVE A... UH... **FLING** WITH A WOMAN WHOSE **HISTORY** I WAS UNSURE OF...

A **ONE-NIGHT STAND**? A CHEAP, TAWDRY ENCOUNTER? **YOU**? MO, I'M SHOCKED!

I WAS YOUNG AND **FOOLISH**! IT WAS MY **FIRST TIME** IN A WOMEN'S BAR... I THOUGHT IT WAS **REQUIRED BEHAVIOR**! SHE **SEDUCED** ME AND I NEVER **SAW** HER AGAIN!

HOW BITTERSWEET. MO, **RELAX**! IT'S NO BIG **DEAL**!

BUT IT **IS**! I DON'T KNOW ANYTHING **ABOUT** HER! **TECHNICALLY**, THAT MAKES ME **HIGH RISK**!

LISTEN... EVEN **KNOWING** PEOPLE'S HISTORIES DOESN'T GUARANTEE ANYTHING... EVEN SUPPOSING YOU **KNOW** WHO ALL YOUR LOVERS' **OTHER** PARTNERS HAVE BEEN, HOW DO YOU KNOW WHO **THEY'VE** SLEPT WITH? OR WHO **THEIR LOVERS** HAVE SLEPT WITH?! IT'S PRACTICALLY **IMPOSSIBLE**!

YEAH.. **JEEZ**, Y'KNOW, IF YOU **THINK** ABOUT IT, THERE'S NOTHING TO DO BUT CRAWL INTO A GIANT ZIP-LOCK **BAGGIE** AND RETIRE TO A **CONVENT**!

THAT'S NOT TRUE! YOU'RE SUCH AN **ALARMIST**! I CAN THINK OF **LOTS** OF THINGS WE COULD DO.

YEAH, RIGHT. LIKE HAVE SEX OVER THE **TELEPHONE**?

ACTUALLY, **KISSING** IS RELATIVELY LOW RISK...

WHAT? UH... I MEAN...

YOU'RE ADORABLE WHEN YOU **PANIC**. I BET YOU SAY THAT TO ALL THE GIRLS.

Libby reid

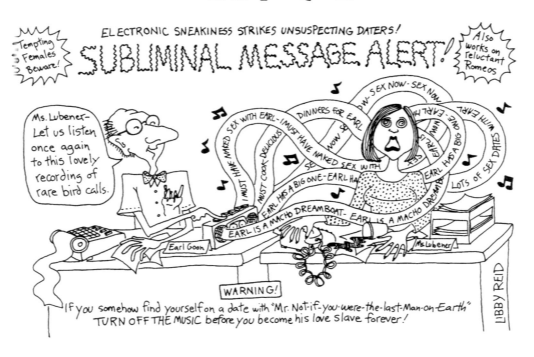

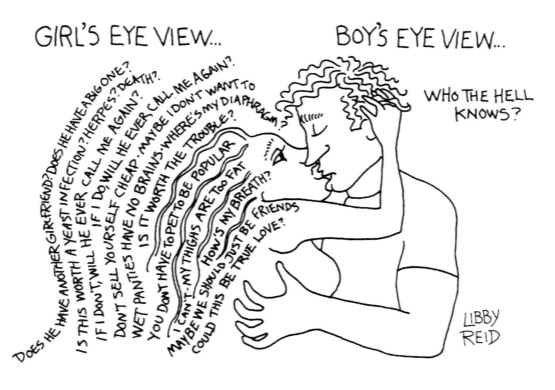

jennifer camper

jennifer camper

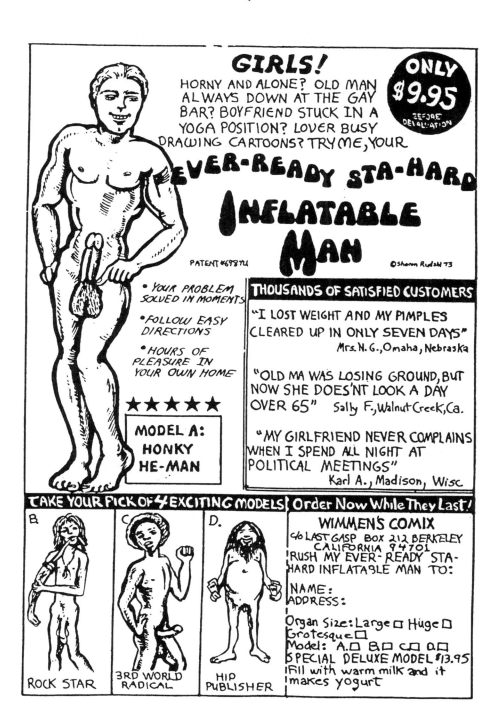

cath jackson

People don't have sex anymore. It is too dangerous. It can kill you. Instead, people watch. They watch movies, t.v., videos.

Sometimes they watch movies about having sex, but this precipitates actually wanting to have sex...

So, mostly, they watch other things...

" Sex? With you?" she scoffed...
"I'd sooner have Ray Charles perform
Root Surgery...."

Before retiring... she liked a glass
of wine, a good book and a Virile Man...

"I've had worse relationships..."
She thought

" Oh, look. There's Bill, Jesse and Tony. Or, as I think of them... the appetizer, the main course, and dessert ... "

He was the kind of guy you
Could write home about...
If your Parents were into
booze, drugs and cheap Sex...

"I Call it bore-play.
That's when he spends
3 hours touching you...
in the wrong Place!"

According to a recent world wide Scientific survey of the sexes... It was determined that there is a real difference in the reasons...

why women have Sex...

It is the ultimate expression of my deepest, most innermost feelings for the person with whom I'm involved in a Permanent or Semi-Permanent relationship

Why Men have Sex...

Because it feels good! uh... And I Sleep better! That's the Scientific Part!

Strip T's by Stephanie ©90

Linda Sue Welch

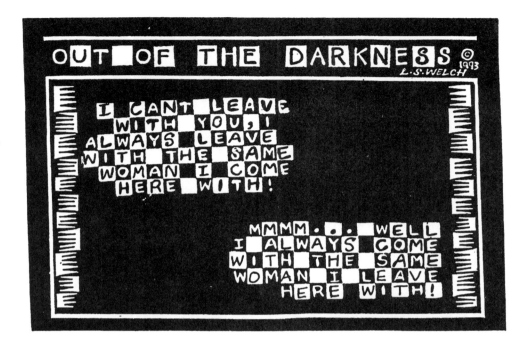

fernanda core

FERNANDA
1989 CORE

fernanda core

*He isn't a Montegue.
First woman: Yes, Yes that was the first with Paolo.
Second woman: ...and then?

Then he looked at me and said, "Did you come?"

And I said, "Well…yes…it was okay…but you could ask me if I liked it…it isn't only a question of coming."

And the other times he asked me, "Did you come?"

And I said that I wasn't a pressure cooker that whistled when through…that it isn't just a question of coming.

And on the 275th time he asked, "Did you come?"

And I said…

shary flenniken

continued…

continued...

continued...

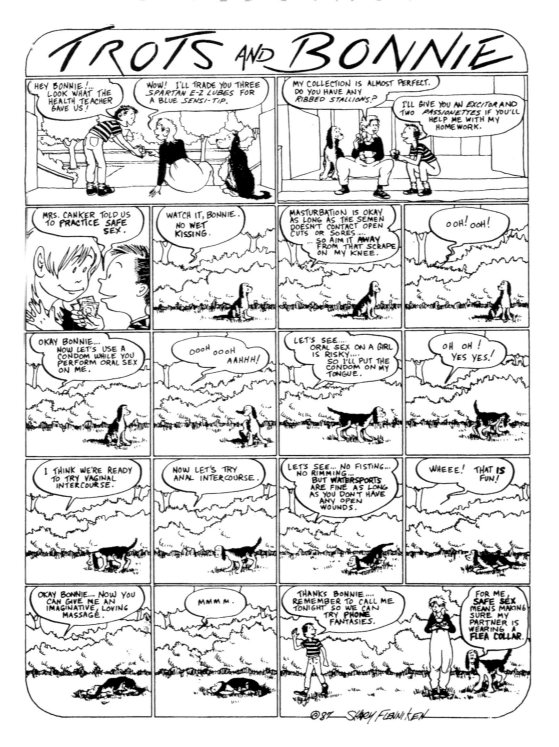

Shary Flenniken

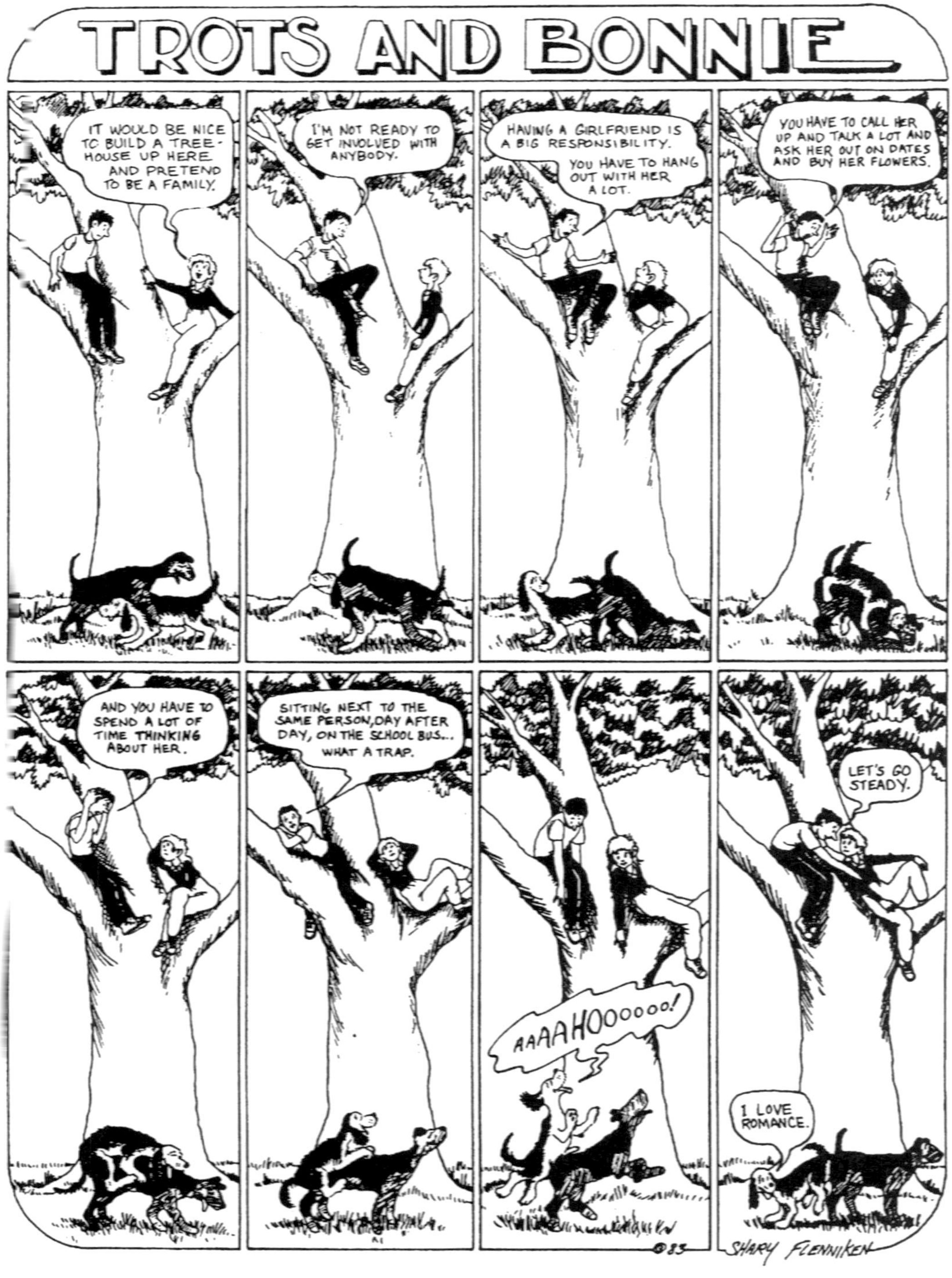

dianne diMassa

THE TRAGEDY OF afrAIDS

a public cervix announcement from Nina Paley

WHAT IS afrAIDS?

afrAIDS IS THE OFTEN IRRATIONAL FEAR OF AIDS.

R.I.P. NINA ... DIDN'T KEEP HER PANTS ZIPPED

© 1-93

continued...

NINA PALEY

HOW THE afrAIDS VIRUS WORKS:

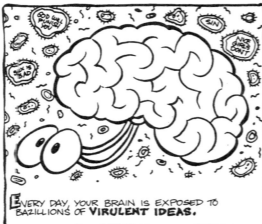

Every day, your brain is exposed to bazillions of **VIRULENT IDEAS.**

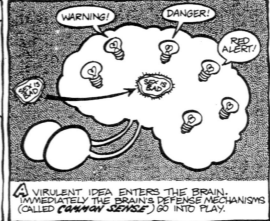

A virulent idea enters the brain. Immediately the brain's defense mechanisms (called *COMMON SENSE*) go into play.

The virulent idea is attacked by common sense, thus destroyed before it can infect the entire system.

The afrAIDS virus, however, "fools" your brain's defense mechanisms.

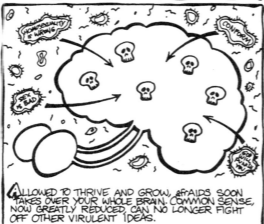

Allowed to thrive and grow, afrAIDS soon takes over your whole brain. Common sense, now greatly reduced, can no longer fight off other virulent ideas.

Eventually you become a paranoid idiot.

continued...

WHO CAN GET afrAIDS?

THE afrAIDS VIRUS WAS FIRST DISCOVERED IN CERTAIN "HIGH-RISK" GROUPS, INCLUDING:

- CATHOLICS
- FUNDAMENTALISTS
- HOMOPHOBES
- REPUBLICANS

IT'S TRUE— I HAVE afrAIDS!!

EWW! DON'T GIVE IT TO ME!

HOWEVER, THE afrAIDS EPIDEMIC HAS SPREAD SO RAPIDLY THAT RECENT STUDIES SHOW

EVERYONE IS NOW AT RISK!

HOW IS afrAIDS TRANSMITTED? afrAIDS IS TRANSMITTED THROUGH CERTAIN "HIGH-RISK" ACTIVITIES, INCLUDING EXPOSURE TO THE FOLLOWING:

TELEVISION

SEX=DEATH
KEEP YOUR PANTS ZIPPED!
—a message from this station

Newsweek?
CELIBACY IS BACK!
KEEP YOUR PANTS ZIPPED!

The Modern Girl's Guide to KEEPING YOUR PANTS ZIPPED

BOOKS

MAGAZINES

RADIO

HONEY, KEEP YOUR PANTS ZIPPED♪ BABY, DON'T YOU LIE ♪ DARLIN', LET'S GET MARRIED♪♪ OR WE'RE BOTH GONNA DIE♪

RELIGIOUS SERVICES

NEWSPAPERS

The Daily Rag
DEATH
DEATH
EXPERTS SAY: KEEP YOUR PANTS ZIPPED
DEATH

...AND THE LORD SAID, "THOU SHALT KEEP THY PANTS ZIPPED."

WHILE EXPOSURE TO THE ABOVE DOES NOT GUARANTEE INFECTION, IT IS BEST TO **ALWAYS USE PROTECTION** WHEN BEING FUCKED BY THE MEDIA OR ENGAGING IN SOCIAL INTERCOURSE.

continued…

WHAT ARE THE SYMPTOMS OF afrAIDS?

- TERROR
- ANXIETY
- GUILT
- RENEWED INTEREST IN RELIGION
- ISOLATION
- SEE LIFE FLASH BEFORE EYES AFTER SEX
- SELF-RIGHTEOUSNESS
- CELIBACY

HI, MY NAME'S—

AAAUGH!!

HOW CAN I PROTECT MYSELF?

- FIRST, OBVIOUSLY, PRACTICE "SAFE SEX."

DUH!

- SOME PEOPLE ARE TOO SCARED OF **AIDS** TO ENGAGE IN **ANY** KIND OF SEX, EVEN WITH PRECAUTIONS. FOR SUCH INDIVIDUALS WE RECOMMEND OTHER, NONSEXUAL ACTIVITIES THAT POSE NO RISK OF **AIDS** WHATSOEVER.

THE FOLLOWING ACTIVITIES WILL **NOT** GIVE YOU AIDS:

- BUNGEE JUMPING
- DRAG RACING
- JUMPING OFF A BRIDGE
- SNAKE MILKING
- PLAYING IN TRAFFIC
- RUNNING FULL SPEED INTO BRICK WALLS
- SKYDIVING

*ARE YOU **SURE** I CAN'T GET AIDS FROM JUMPING OFF A BRIDGE?*

TO PROTECT YOURSELF FROM afrAIDS, WE RECOMMEND:

MEDIA CONDOMS & MENTAL DAMS

THESE METHODS ARE EVEN **MORE** EFFECTIVE WHEN USED WITH OTHER FORMS OF PROTECTION. FOR EXAMPLE, AFTER PLACING THE CONDOM OVER THE TELEVISION, PULL OUT THE PLUG.

WHAT ABOUT THE FUTURE?

TIMES ARE TOUGH FOR THE SEXUALLY ACTIVE, BUT REMEMBER:

THERE IS HOPE!!

AS MEDICAL SCIENCE DISCOVERS A CURE FOR **AIDS**, afrAIDS, TOO, SHALL BE ABOLISHED. ONCE AGAIN WE CAN RETURN TO THOSE HAPPY, CAREFREE DAYS WHEN ALL WE HAD TO WORRY ABOUT WAS UNWANTED PREGNANCY, HERPES, SYPHILIS, GONORRHEA, CHLAMYDIA, CERVICAL CANCER, AND ETERNAL DAMNATION.

HAVE A NICE DAY!

THE END!

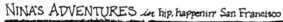

NINA PALEY

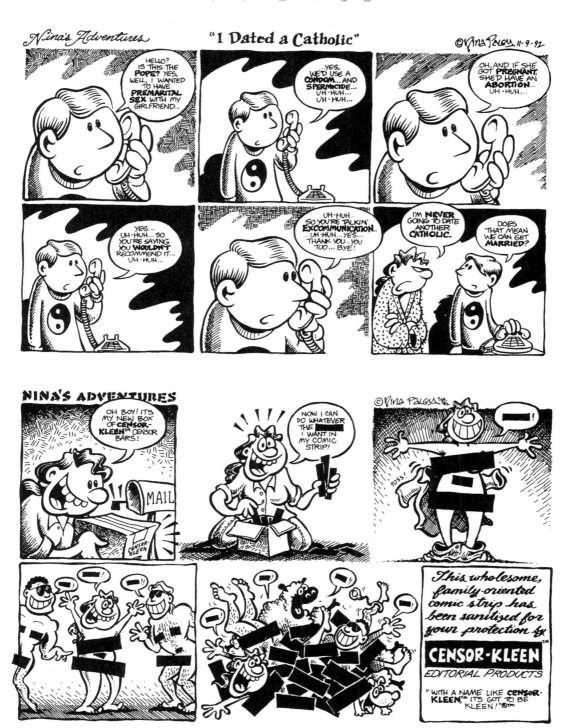

"SAFE SEX! SAFE SEX! THAT'S ALL YOU THINK ABOUT!"

Margie cherry

barbara brandon

Lee Kennedy

continued...

Lee Kennedy

Hungry for information about him, I blew pocket money on trashy movie magazines...

If anyone saw me buying this stuff, I'd be MORTIFIED, but I gotta have that COLOUR pic!

One day I discovered something that SHATTERED me...

⟨MARRIED!⟩ ...to beautiful actress (oh god, she IS...) Jill Ireland; two CHILDREN!

WHINE

I wept in the basement all afternoon!

I'd been taught that wanting to sin was as bad as actually doing it. This made me an ⋮ALDULTERESS⋮

I tried escaping "occasions of sin" by avoiding the mags, and "Man From U.N.C.L.E."

Immaculate Mary, Keep me Pure...

SNIVEL

COME BACK, LUV!

It was no use; my phantom passion was strong...

SMOOCH

Must have been all of 15, and didn't even know how to masturbate!

I'm a lost soul, a fallen woman... but I LOVE HIM!

I "Lost the Faith" over David McCallum!

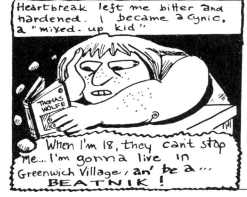

Heartbreak left me bitter and hardened. I became a cynic, a "mixed-up kid"

THOMAS WOLFE

When I'm 18, they can't stop me... I'm gonna live in Greenwich Village, an' be a... BEATNIK!

I became mentally promiscuous, planning to 'do it' with any number of celebrities I was unlikely to ever meet. (I never had a 'date' with a boy throughout High School!)

Still ugly and fat, but Albert Finney is sure to love me for my soul...

⋮SIGH⋮

WHITE LIPSTICK

In secret, I made myself up...

continued...

Sometimes I'd manage to sneak into Manhattan. put on my slap and 'Beat' gear, and do the Art Museums. Occasionally, men would come on to me, but though I was keen to be free of my virginity, they were always just _too_ grotesque!

Don't be so shy... I'm interested in you.
I don't judge by looks etc. etc.
Oh GOD!

At last, I escaped, to a 'Non-Catholic' college. It was Co-Ed... There I met an exotic Jewish boy, who was blatantly gay, but I couldn't work this out...

I.... LOVE you!
RANT
CLUTCH
And I love you ... like my own sister!

Certain that this lack of passion was _entirely_ due to my unsightliness, I grew even more bitter & twisted, and drank heavily...

why am I CURSED? ¿snuk¿

GLUB

At last, I scored with a stoned, but presentable Polish Sailor at a wild party...

BOG
My waters 'ave broken!
RATTLE
Who the fux IN there?
THE PIGS are comin! I know they're here ALREADY!
I'm freakin' out
RUTH!

We were in the bathtub for nearly two hours...

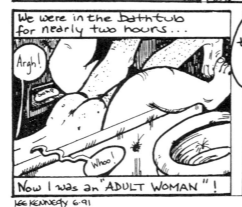

Argh!
Whoo!

Now I was an "ADULT WOMAN"!

LEE KENNEDY 6·91

Unfortunately, I really enjoyed it, and went on to a string of totally DEGRADED, emotionally masochistic affairs, not to mention all the sleazy one-night stands... AND pathetic crushes...

And, would ja credit it? I _still_ kinda believe in ROMANCE ♡
SNORT

roberta gregory

continued…

continued...

continued...

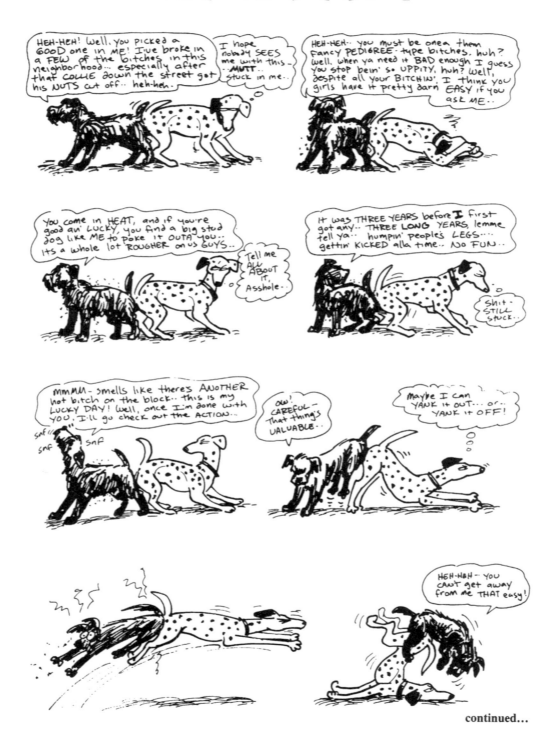

continued...

roberta gregory

Bedroom Politricks

©1980 Roberta Gregory

continued...

continued…

continued...

continued...

wendy eastwood

continued…

wendy eastwood

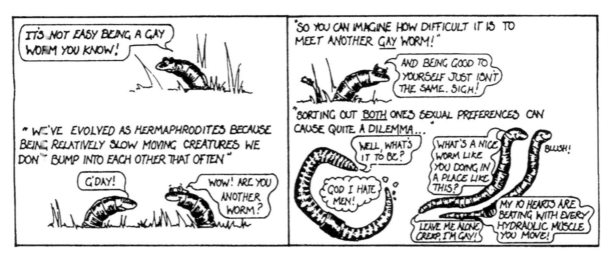

kris kovick

AT THE STROKE OF MIDNIGHT CINDERELLA'S PUSSY TURNS INTO A PUMPKIN. AS SHE'S RUSHING HOME, SHE MEETS THE PRINCE.

kris kovick

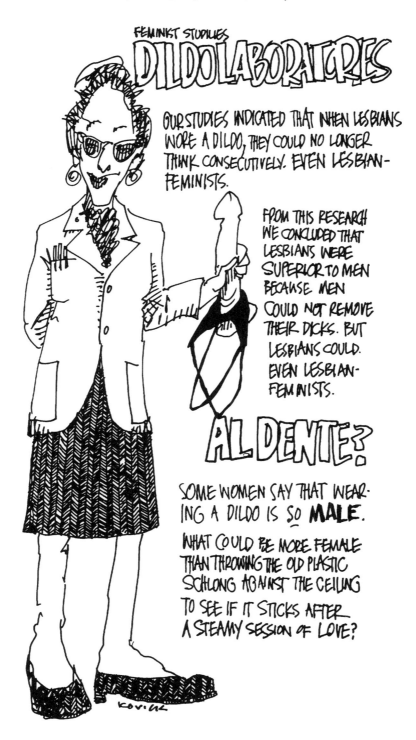

FEMINIST STUDIES

DILDOLABORATORIES

OUR STUDIES INDICATED THAT WHEN LESBIANS WORE A DILDO, THEY COULD NO LONGER THINK CONSECUTIVELY. EVEN LESBIAN-FEMINISTS.

FROM THIS RESEARCH WE CONCLUDED THAT LESBIANS WERE SUPERIOR TO MEN BECAUSE MEN COULD NOT REMOVE THEIR DICKS. BUT LESBIANS COULD. EVEN LESBIAN-FEMINISTS.

AL DENTE?

SOME WOMEN SAY THAT WEARING A DILDO IS SO **MALE**.

WHAT COULD BE MORE FEMALE THAN THROWING THE OLD PLASTIC SCHLONG AGAINST THE CEILING

TO SEE IF IT STICKS AFTER A STEAMY SESSION OF LOVE?

KOVICK

HOW TO DISTINGUISH BETWEEN ACTS OF PASSION & LESS SERIOUS FLIRTATIONS

IT WASN'T REALLY INTIMATE...

☐ SHE WORE RUBBER GLOVES
☐ SHE USED HER LEFT HAND
☐ SHE USED A VEGETABLE

TOE CLEAVAGE

THE ULTIMATE TURN-ON FOR SOME.

THE POOR WOMAN'S VIBRATOR

THE BILL of RIGHTS IS OUR MOST EFFECTIVE SEX TOY!

nicole ferentz

SHE DREAMED OF LIVING IN A HUGE APARTMENT WITH
A DIFFERENT LOVER IN EVERY ROOM.

jacki randall

..,DEVOTION..

GAYNOR CARDEW

GAYNOR

barbary o'brien

jane caminos

signe wilkinson

catherine goggia

giuliana maldini

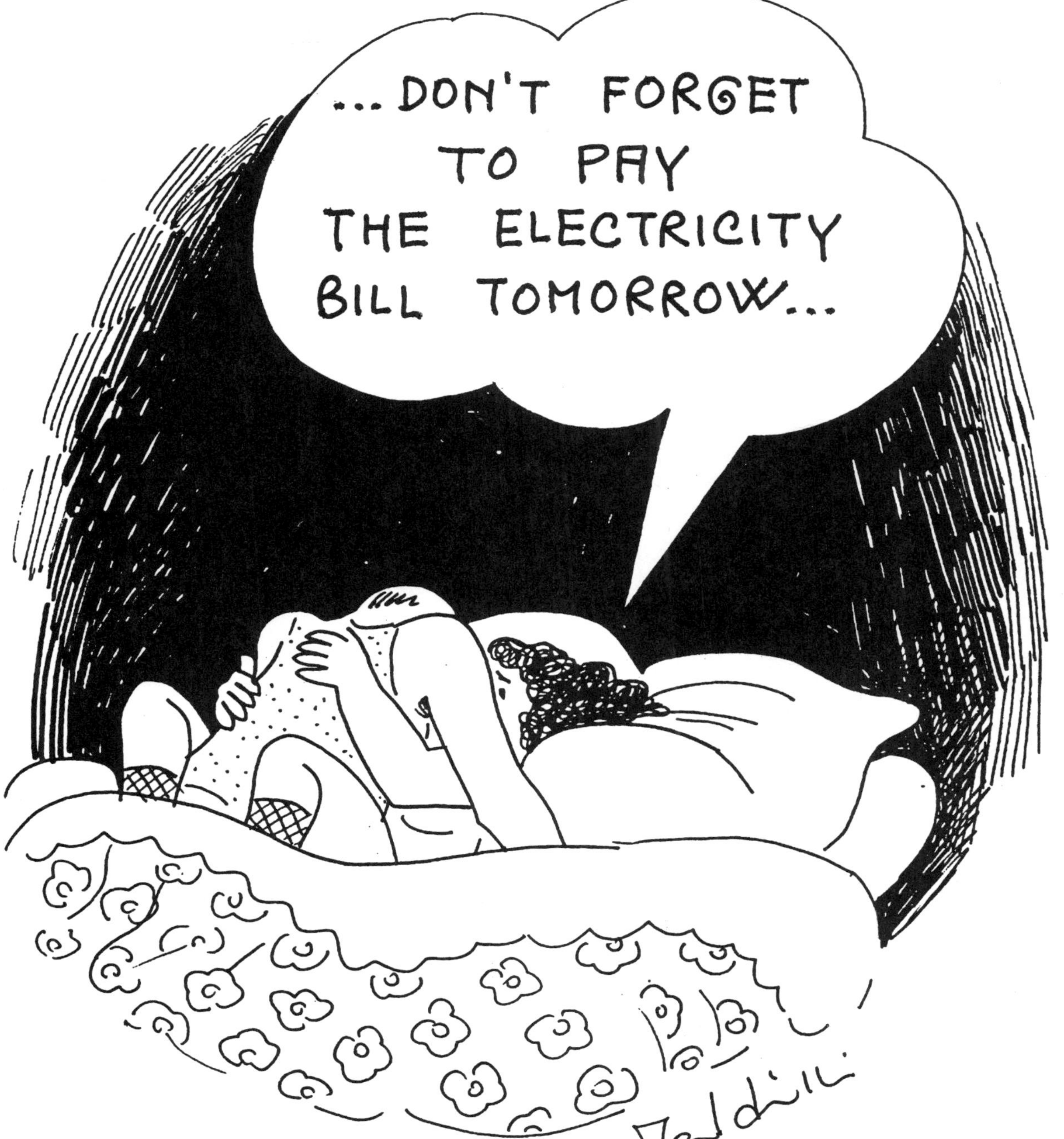
...DON'T FORGET
TO PAY
THE ELECTRICITY
BILL TOMORROW...

The faces of these women are hidden and their voices altered to protect their identities

DYKE SEX RAP

© Noreen Stevens '90

HI, I'M ALKON. I'VE NEVER TOLD ANYONE THIS BUT I'VE ALWAYS ENVIED THE HONEST APPROACH GAY MEN HAVE TOWARD ANONYMOUS SEX

WHERE I LIVE THERE'S THIS SPOT ALONG THE RIVER WHERE MEN CRUISE AND HAVE SEX IN THE BUSHES

CAN YOU IMAGINE WALKING THROUGH THE WOODS AT NIGHTFALL, HEARING MOVEMENT AROUND YOU & KNOWING ITS THE SOUND OF WOMEN **HAVING SEX**?

I SEE THE SILHOUETTE OF A WOMAN LEANING AGAINST A TREE. WALKING UP TO HER I TOUCH HER BREASTS THROUGH HER T-SHIRT. IT'S WHAT I WANT—IT'S WHAT SHE WANTS. ITS ALL SO **UNCOMPLICATED!!**

MY NAME IS JANINE. I FIRST MET MY GIRLFRIEND BECAUSE SHE DID FOOT PATROL—SHE'S A POLICE OFFICER—THROUGH THE PARK WHERE I ALWAYS EAT MY LUNCH. I'D FORGET HOW TO CHEW WHEN SHE WALKED BY, SHE WAS SO BEAUTIFUL...

I CAME HOME ONE NIGHT A FEW MONTHS AGO AND THERE SHE WAS IN FULL UNIFORM. SHE STARTED TO KISS ME AND TAKE OFF MY CLOTHES WITHOUT A WORD THE WHOLE TIME... IT WAS THE BEST SEX EVER!

IT WASN'T THE AUTHORITY FIGURE THAT TURNED ME ON... WHAT I LIKED WAS MAKING LOVE TO HER DRESSED THE WAY SHE WAS WHEN I FIRST MET HER...

OR MAYBE IT **WAS** THE **AUTHORITY THING** TOO... MAYBE THAT'S WHAT ATTRACTED ME IN THE FIRST PLACE?! WHO KNOWS?

47

MORE! DYKE SEX RAP

The faces of these women are hidden and their voices altered to protect their identities

MY NAME IS MARION. THE ONE THING I REALLY MISS ABOUT SEX WITH MY HUSBAND...

IS THE WAY IT FELT WHEN HE WAS INSIDE ME. I WISH MY LOVER WAS MORE INTO THAT—EVEN USING HER FINGERS...

I SUGGESTED WE TRY A CUCUMBER ONCE BUT SHE LAUGHED IN MY FACE—SAID SHE ISN'T INTO VEGETABLES...

SHE'D DIE IF SHE HEARD ME SAY THIS BUT ONCE, JUST ONCE I'D LIKE TO BE FUCKED LIKE THAT BY HER... NAILED TO THE MATTRESS, Y'KNOW JUST...

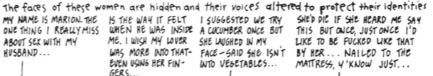

HI, SORRY I'M LATE... HEY, WHY ARE THE LIGHTS OFF?... IS IT MY TURN? OKAY, MY NAME'S MICHELE. MY GIRLFRIEND AND I LIKE TO GO TO THE BEACH AND MAKE LOVE. IT'S NOT LIKE WE DO IT IN FRONT OF PEOPLE OR ANYTHING...

BUT THEY'RE AROUND. PART OF THE GAME IS TRYING TO GET CAUGHT... SOMETIMES WE DO, TOO. WE'RE A BIT NOISY, WHICH HELPS...

AND YOU SHOULD SEE THE LOOKS ON THEIR FACES—ESPECIALLY WHEN WE DON'T EVEN STOP WHAT WE'RE DOING. WE REALLY GET OFF ON THAT...

WHAT ARE Y'ALL LOOKING AT? WHAT ROOM IS THIS? DID I ACCIDENTALLY WALK INTO THE A.A. MEETING?

© Noreen Stevens '90

Lynn Johnston

HMPH. WATCH HOW SHE FLIRTS WITH MICHAEL!

THEY'RE JUST TALKING, EL.

COME ON! - IT'S THE WAY SHE MOVES, THE WAY SHE SPEAKS! - LOOK AT HER BODY LANGUAGE!

WHEN I WAS THEIR AGE, I NEVER DID THINGS LIKE THAT!

... OF COURSE, I NEVER HAD THE BODY OR THE LANGUAGE!

I THINK THOSE TWO ARE GETTING ENTIRELY TOO FRIENDLY.

THEY'RE JUST KIDS, EL.

THEY'RE 15! THEY MIGHT BE JUST KIDS, JOHN, BUT THEIR PARTS ARE ALL WORKING AND THEIR MINDS ARE IN GEAR!

THE FEAR IS, THEY'LL TRY OPERATING THE EQUIPMENT WITHOUT READING THE MANUAL.

rhonda dickfion

ARTSY BOOKS ALWAYS MADE
GAYLE AND ABBY
FEEL SOMEHOW INADEQUATE.

You took the batteries out of the vibrator and put them in the remote. Is this a comment on our love life?

I DON'T MIND IF THE CATS WATCH–
BUT NO FOREPAW!

joann palanker

Yesterday Jenny and I had our little talk about the facts of life. I simply told her, honey, sex with the right man is a beautiful thing.

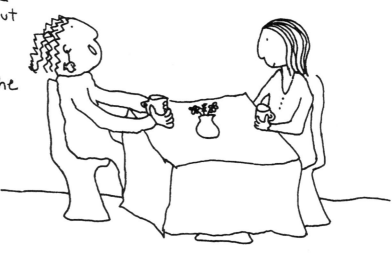

I thought I'd leave out that sex with the wrong man is pretty great too.

claire bretecher

There's no way that I'm going to slip up I've got a new anodized uranium I.U.D ... I take the Japanese day-after pill ... I got three packets of condoms by my bed

I'm very together about it

especially since just after my hysterectomy I met Lucy

jan eliot

WONDER GIRL SURVEYS THE LANDSCAPE. ALL IS QUIET IN THIS CORNER OF THE WORLD THAT SHE PROTECTS WITH WISDOM AND JUSTICE.

WHO IS SHE? WHERE DID SHE COME FROM? NO ONE KNOWS FOR SURE...

WHILE SOME SPREAD RUMORS OF A GROSSLY CLINICAL NATURE, TRUE BELIEVERS HANG ON TO THE CABBAGE PATCH THEORY...

GROSS! YUCK!! YOU'VE GOT TO BE KIDDING!!

MAYBE IT'S A LITTLE EARLY FOR THIS...

Maggie Ling

contributors' Notes

Alison Bechdel's "Dykes to Watch Out For" cartoon strip is syndicated in 45 feminist, gay, lesbian and progressive newspapers in the United States and Canada. Four collections of her cartoons—*Dykes to Watch Out For, More Dykes to Watch out For, New, Improved! Dykes to Watch Out For, and Dykes to Watch Out For; The Sequel*—as well as a yearly calendar, have been published by Firebrand Books (141 The Commons, Ithaca, NY 14850). She was a contributor to *Women's Glib, Women's Glibber* and *Kitty Libber*. Bechdel currently lives in Vermont.

Suzy Becker is the author of the national best-seller *All I Need to Know I Learned from My Cat* and of *The All Better Book*. She also founded and runs The Widget Factory, a greeting card company in New England, where she lives with her Holstein cat, Binky.

Barbara Brandon is the only African American female cartoonist currently published in a major U.S. newspaper. Her "Where I'm Coming From" has appeared in the lifestyle pages of *The Detroit Free Press* since June 1989. Universal Press Syndicate is now syndicating her strip nationally. A 1980 graduate of SU's College of Visual and Performing Arts, Brandon has previously worked as a fashion and beauty writer for *Essence* magazine, and as an illustrator for *Essence*, the *Crisis*, the *Village Voice* and MCA Records. She resides in New York.

Jane Caminos is a Brooklyn native, but grew up in New Jersey. She graduated from the Rhode Island School of Design in 1969 and moved to Boston where she began a long, successful career as a designer and illustrator, first in book publishing management and later as an independent. In 1991 she moved her personal life and her business, Illustratus, to Tribeca in New York City. Caminos is also a talented painter who has had numerous one-woman exhibitions of her art. She says that she used to paint "only for relaxation and to combat the rules imposed by commercial work," but in the late 1980s she was convinced by the owner of a gallery in Brookline, MA to show her work publicly. Since then, her paintings, which *The Boston Globe* called "vivid," have been exhibited in galleries and public spaces throughout Eastern Massachusetts and New York. Caminos says she "came out in the mid-1970s when it was not politically correct to have a sense of humor, and has been waiting all these years for lesbian life to loosen up enough so she could publish" her work.

Jennifer Camper lives in New York City. Her biweekly cartoon, "Camper," runs nationally in lesbian and gay publications. Her work has also appeared in *Gay Comix, Wimmin's Comix, On Our Backs, Young Lust, Strip Aids, Choices, Women's Glib, Women's Glibber* and *Kitty Libber*. Her hobbies include garlic, fast cards and large-breasted women.

Gaynor Cardew started drawing cartoons as a way to remember those dinner party jokes for which she was notorious for forgetting the punch line. She was born in the early fifties in a small central Queensland (Australia) town as a result of her parents trying to get it right after the birth of her elder brother. (They eventually gave up after the fifth attempt, although they enjoyed the practice.) She works freelance for unions and government agencies trying to explain often very dry work-related issues in cartoon form. Her hobbies are cooking, eating, drinking and drawing comics on women's fantasies.

Margie Cherry, cartoonist-writer-mom, is planning to have wild, carefree, spontaneous sex in the year 2000 when both her daughters will be old enough for overnight camp. Meanwhile she's training them to watch three videos in a row so she and her husband can sneak upstairs for a quickie. When she's not fantasizing about sex, Margie can be found in her studio creating her cartoon, "The Art of Motherhood" which appears in a local parenting publication. Her work has appeared in the cartoon anthology *Mothers*. Inspiration for her cartoons are provided by Sasha, 5, Dana, 2 1/2, and Ivan, 38. They live together in a crazy, colorful, chaotic old house outside Philadelphia.

Fernanda Core lives in Milan where she works as a painter and humor designer. She is part of the Milan group "Humor Graphic". In 1978 she founded, together with other women artists, the magazine *Strix*, which was the sole Italian comic magazine by and for women.

Having learned the skills necessary for survival in her home state of Washington ("Mud boots are not good for dancing!") **Rhonda Dicksion** has gone on to author *The Lesbian Survival Manual* (Naiad Press, 1990) and contribute to numerous books and publications. Her next ambitious projects include her book *Stay Tooned* (Naiad Press, 1993) and learning how to drive in the snow.

Patrizia de Ambrogio was born in 1952 and obtained a degree in Architecture in 1977 in Milan where she taught and began her artistic activities. Since 1985 she has worked for a ceramic laboratory and also in a puppet theatre where she designs and makes scenery. Her work has appeared in a number of shows and has won many prizes.

Diane Dimassa is the creator of "Hothead Paisan—Homicidal Lesbian Terrorist" the quarterly comic-zine, which will appear in Fall 1993 as a real live book/anthology by Cleis Press. Look for it, buy it, love it, give it to everyone. Thanks. (Note: Editor Roz Warren is the founder of "Hets for Hothead" a terrorist auxiliary fanclub which is legal in most jurisdictions. For more information contact Roz.

Wendy Eastwood Born 1964, I was brought up in Gloucester, a beautiful county in the heart of the British countryside where lesbians are so invisible that they can't even see themselves! I ran away to study architecture in London, and after my degree I worked for an interior design company for three years, but gave it up because I was more interested in drawing people than the seats they sat in and the buildings they lived in. In 1989 at the request of the editor I drew my first cartoon for the Christmas issue of Britain's Gay and Lesbian newspaper The Pink Paper. The strip was so well received that I was asked to continue. I live in London with my lover and cat, Fluffy.

Jan Eliot lives in Eugene, Oregon, and is a motherhood survivor. While her two handsome daughters make their own way in the world, she pursues her somewhat illusive cartoon career. For comic relief from the fun of reading rejection slips (as well as for actual money) Jan creates and writes advertising. Next to her husband Ted, Jan thanks Roz for her support. See Jan's cartoons in *Women's Glibber*, *The 1993 Women's Glib Engagement Calendar* and *Mothers!* (The Crossing Press).

Nicole Ferentz is an artist/illustrator/greeting card creator/teacher/graphic designer and most recently, letterer, living and working in Chicago. In other words, a Jill-of-all Trades living in a time of post-industrial specialization. She illustrated Celeste West's *Lesbian Love Advisor* (Cleis Press $9.95). Her own books include

The 1989 Working Girl's Datebook (self published $9.95). *Perky Boo-Boo, Pesky Boo-Boo* (self-published $15.00) and *Recovering From Cancer at Home* (self-published $15.00)

FISH "I've published stuff in *Anything That Moves, Bad Attitude, Betty & Pansy's Severe Queer Review, The Black Book, Frighten the Horses, Locomotive, Outlook* and *Rites.* I also publish *Brat Attack; The Zine for Leatherdykes and other Bad Girls* which has lots of cartoons in it. (It's available for $4 from POB 40754, San Francisco, CA 94140—include an age statement!)

Cartoonist, screenwriter and former National Lampoon magazine editor **Shary Flenniken** lives in Seattle, Washington and likes to work in her garden, turning over rocks to find the crawly things underneath.

Ellen Forney recently came out as a cartoonist, and occasionally leaves her drawing board to swim, dance, eat and sleep. Her work has appeared in *MS., Naughty Bits, Real Smart* and *The Rocket.*

Leanne Franson "A one-time prarie anglophobe, I am now a bilingual easterner in Montreal, where I do my best to provide financial aid to the neighborhood copy centre, Canada Post and Bell Canada. For inspiration I do Swedish massage, run a bi women's group and hang out in gay bars. I drew cartoons in 1986 for one month until I fell in love. "Liliane" comix were reborn in March 1992. My ambition now is to have my work appear in a publication I can show to my grandmother. Publication credits include *OH, Strange-looking Exile, GirlJock, Brat Attack* and Gay Comics." ("Liliane" minicomix are available for $1.50 each from: Leanne Franson, 3908 St. Christophe, Montreal, Quebec, Canada H2L 3X8.)

Catherine Goggia lives in Chico, California. She has a bachelor's degree in visual communication and in English. Catherine's cartoons have appeared in newspapers, on T-shits and buttons, in healthcare educational publications, and the *Women's Glib 1993* calendar, just to name a few places. She illustrated and co-wrote a counseling workbook and even had some poetry published on a particularly expressive day. Catherine's blessed consistent income is derived from employment as a motivational speaker. She is also a freelance graphic designer and photographer. Sometimes Catherine sells her cartoons door to door—whatever it takes to continue writing and drawing! Cartoonist hero figure: Lynda Barry.

Roberta Gregory has been doing her best to infiltrate the male-dominated comic book world since 1974. She has been a regular contributor to *Wimmen's Comix* and *Gay Comics* and now has a regularly published series, *Naughty Bits,* available from Fantagraphics Books (7563 Lake City Way NE Seattle, Washington 98115). Her own self-published work, including the groundbreaking *Dynamite Damsels* (1976), the acclaimed *Artistic Licentiousness* (1991) plus *Sheila and the Unicorn* and *Winging It* can be ordered through her catalogue, available for a SASE from Roberta Gregory, Box 27438, Seattle, Washington 98125. Her work was featured in *Kitty Libber, Women's Glibber* and *Mothers!.*

Marion Henley's comic strip, "Maxine," is distributed by Carmen Syndicate. Her work has also appeared in many publications whose target audiences run the gamut: Russian feminists, industrial psychologists, "at-risk" teenaged girls, stutterers, recovering scientologists, and (significantly) Hawaiian polygamists. As for sex, she has never managed to get the truth out of her mother, who will only admit that "dogs do it."

Nicole Hollander's "Sylvia" comic strip is syndicated to 46 newspapers. Her work is collected in *Tales from the Planet Sylvia, The Whole Enchilada* and others. Her work was featured in *Women's Glib.*

Judy Horacek is an Australian cartoonist and writer based in Melbourne. Her work has been widely published in women's, alternative and community publications and she produces a range of postcards and greeting cards. Unrequited Love is one of her favorite topics. *Life on the Edge,* a collection of her cartoons, is available through Spinifex Press (ph. Melbourne 329 6088, P.O. Box 212, North Melbourne, Vic 3051, Australia).

Cath Jackson lives and works in London. She has published two collections of her cartoons—*Wonder Wimbin* (Battle Axe Books, 1984) and *Visibly Vera* (Women's Press, 1986). Her work appears regularly in the UK radical feminist magazine *Trouble & Strife*.

Lynn Johnson has won numerous awards, including the Reuben award for Outstanding Cartoonist of the Year (the first and only woman to win this award) from the National Cartoonists Society (NCS) and Best Syndicated Comic Strip (*For Better or For Worse*) from the NCS. Johnston's home is Ontario, Canada, where she lives with husband Rod and children, Aaron and Katie.

Lee Kennedy A life long cartoonist and comix freak. After a thrillingly dysfunctional childhood packed with frightening Irish Catholic guilt trips in the bleak suburbs of Long Island, she opted for La Vie de Boheme and ended up an "inner city pagan" in London. Now a crabby old fat lady, she scratches a marginal living as a telephonist, devoting every possible moment to her tormented depictions of tortured angst. *Still* dreams of becoming a star and making a living from her 'aht'! Work appears in *Kitty Libber, Fanny, Girl Frenzy* and others. She can be reached at: 58 Durrington/Westbury Wandsworth Road/London SW8 3LF/England.

Kris Kovick is a cartoonist and writer in San Francisco. Her two books, *What I Love About Lesbian Politics is Arguing With People I Agree With* and *What If Your Dad Was Gay* were nominated for Lambda Book Awards for 1991, one in the slut category, the other in children's books. Her work was featured in *Women's Glibber* and *Mothers!*, and she will illustrate *GlibQuips: Funny Words by Funny Women* (Crossing Press, 1994).

Kathryn LeMieux has done award-winning editorial cartoons for the Pt. Reyes Light and the Marin Independent Journal. She also did the comic strip "Lyttle Women" for King Features Syndicate. She lives in West Marin County with her husband and son.

Shan Leslie "I have basically one response to life's difficulties, humor. This has been a major support system throughout my life. I was born in 1940 and even before school age was drawing and sketching. I won a national *Draw Me Girl* contest in 1953. But most of the art I did centered around the old west, until 1984, when I came out as a Lesbian. Cartooning, for me, was a way to release my own feelings and to laugh at the world around me. Since then my work has appeared in *Scene Magazine, Just Out, The LCP* and *The Lavender Network*. Besides cartooning, I still do Native American Paintings, draw and sketch in pen & ink and computer graphics where I create wimmin oriented clip art."

Maggie Ling A post war "bullish" baby, circa May 1948. Weaned from a diet of full cream milk, roast beef and the notion of marital bliss with the perfect homo sap to soya beans, mushroom loaf and fat-free lovers! Rejoices in the fact that, approaching 45, she has no marriages/divorces to feel regretful/guilty about. And despite earlier meternal warnings of depleted energy and sex drive with age, is currently doing very nicely thank you! A collection of Ling's work, *One Woman's Eye (A Wry Look at Life)* was published by Virgin Books and she has a weekly cartoon feature in *The Observer*.

Maureen Lister "I published my first cartoons in our girls' school magazine 25 years ago. My talents then slumbered on undisturbed until 1991, when Luciana Tufani (organiser of the Italian Biennial of Women's Humor *Le Donne Ridono*) pushed and prodded me into doing some work for the exhibition. I also owe a lot to the co-organizers of the first Italian Lesbian Week (1991) whose antics were so wierd and outrageous that all I could do was turn them into cartoons. Since then I've been exhibited at lesbian events in Rome and Berlin, won a competition, and have been published in *Lesbian Contradiction* and other venues. I often work with Silvia who unfailingly shows me the funny side of things and thinks up captions. I earn my living teaching English. My ambition is to earn enough money with cartoons to pay for the stationary.

Gail Machlis' single panel cartoon, *Quality Time*, is distributed by Chronicle Features Syndicate. A collection of her work, *Quality Time and Other Quandries*, is available from Chronicle Books.

Giuliana Maldini e pittrice e disegnatrice umorista e avtrice di vari libri di satira di costume in evi le tematiche predilette ruotano intorno al mondo femminile. Gli ultimi sono "femminiglia" della casa edtrice "Glenat" 1991 e "10 e mia sorella" delle edizioni e. elle 1992 nella collana "Le Letture."

Theresa McCracken is a SWF, thirty-somethingish, biodegradable cartoonist and humor writer. She's homesteading in the Boondocks of Oregon in a leaky trailer that has no electricity. The man of her dreams will have a very long extension cord. When not running deer out of her garden she runs McHumor. Her work has appeared in over 350 magazines, many of them trade journals in dire need of humor. She targets her work to their audiences, be they anemic astronauts or Zen zoologists. She charges $1,000 per hour, but has never been known to take more than 30 seconds to do a drawing or article.

Amy Meredith lives with her 2 cats, dog, girlfriend, mother-in-law, mother-in-law's mother, and girlfriend's niece in Baltimore, Maryland. She's been published here and there, mostly there. She enjoys drawing, reading, stained glass and mediating between the dog and cats.

Andrea Natalie moved to New York from Arizona and came out as a lesbian in 1980. In 1989 she began drawing and syndicating her single-panel cartoon "Stonewall Riots." Her first book, *Stonewall Riots* (Venus Press, 1990) was a Lambda Book Awards finalist and her second book, *The Night Audrey's Vibrator Spoke*, was published by Cleis Press in 1992. She is currently working on her third book.

Barbary O'Brien lives and works in South Australia and practices a very broad definition of the term "artist." She works with young people, in schools, remand centres, health centres, for festivals, retailers, government departments, prisons and local councils on a variety of community art projects. Her cartoons appear in all sorts of odd publications locally and overseas. Her work mostly revolves around the world from a woman's point of view and she has a strong committment to using humour to change perceptions, heal wounds and generally educate. Her cartoons are collected in *Con-sequences* (Wakefield Press, South Australia). When she is not sending up the human race with her cartoons she is probably either gardening, surfing or eating!!

Joann Palanker is a cartoonist living in Los Angeles whose work appears in various Recycled Paper Porducts, Inc. greeting cards. "I'm still trying to find someone I can pay to shave my legs for me." More humorous cards are available through Silly Goose, P.O. Box 25585, Los Angeles, CA 90025-0585. Her work was included in *Women's Glibber* and *Mothers!*.

Nina Paley "America's best-loved unknown cartoonist," was born and raised amidst the cornfields of the Midwest. Nina moved to Santa Cruz, California in 1988 with aspirations of becoming a New Age, crystal-wielding hippie. Instead she became a cynical cartoonist. "The pay's not great, but at least I have my integrity, sort of," says the plucky freelance artist from Illinois. Her work has appeared in numerous books and comics including *Grateful Dead Comics, Women's Glibber, Kitty Libber, Choices, Dark Horse Presents* and many others. Her weekly comic strip "Nina's Adventures" runs in many newspapers. Three terrific collections of her cartoons are available: *Depression is Fun* (T.H.C. Press), *Nina's All-Time Greatest Collector's Item Classic Comics #1* (Dark Horse) and *Nina's Adventures* (Pentshack Press).

Rina Piccolo, a freelance cartoonist and illustrator, has a blister on her finger the size of a grape from drawing too much. Her cartoons have appeared in *Women's Glibber, Kitty Libber,* and *Mothers!.* As an illustrator, her work includes numerous ads, flyers and poster designs, activity booklets for children and some commissioned paintings including a mural. Her cartoons have also appeared in *Comic Relief* magazine, local news magazines and arts journals. Rina has had no formal training except perhaps in high school where her art teacher informed her that cartooning is not an artform. Haw! The blister is getting bigger...

Stephanie H. Piro was born and raised in New York, where she did a lot of things we won't discuss here. She began the Strip T's T Shirt company in 1984, and her work has been licensed to calendar and greeting card companies, has been published in numerous magazines and books including Roz Warren's series of books of women's humor, and *Blank Tapes/Boots and Salads* published by Comic Relief's Page One Publishers. A collection of her 'toons, *Men! Ah!,* is available from Laugh Lines Press. She and her terrific daughter Nico live in Farmington, New Hampshire with Him, a banjo-playing Journalist from Glasgow. For a catalog of over 70 T-shirt and button designs, write to: Strip T's, P.O. Box 605, Farminghton, NH 03835.

Born in Trieste in 1958, **Julia Posar** now lives in Bologna, Italy. An illustrator, she has worked in fashion and publishing. Satirical cartoons are her passion because she loves to use (Italian) words as well as graphics.

Viv Quillin was the youngest and shortest in a family where the larger members liked practising their sexuality on the smaller ones. Her sense of humor has come in handy ever since. She's been a cartoonist for 13 years. "The Opposite Sex" , her fifth book, answers all those questions you got slapped for asking. Her work is also on Christmas cards, post cards and T shirts produced by Cath Tate Cards.

Jacki Randall "I'm up to having 23 tattoos, my work is appearing in *The Bay Area Reporter, Filth Monthly, The Spectator, Brat Attack* and *Odyssey*, as well as having Bay Area showings of my erotic paintings. My first dyke cartoon saw print in *The Baltimore Gaypaper* in 1981."

Libby Reid grew up in the suburbs of Washington, D.C. under the influence of Walt Disney, "Twilight Zone," Beach Blanket movies, Barbie, and of course The Bomb. She now lives in New York where she likes to dwell on her personal problems until they turn into cartoons. For three years, she has been drawing cartoons for her own line of postcards, which are distributed by independent card sales representatives in cities across the country. Her work has appeared in *MS.*, and *The New York Daily News Magazine*, among other publications. Two collections of her work are available from Penguin Books: *Do You Hate Your Hips More Than Nuclear War?* and *You Don't Have to Pet to Be Popular.*

Dianne Reum "Though I was raised in Grants Pass, Oregon, I still haven't totally grown up anywhere. I started cartooning, nonprofessionally, in junior high, when I found that (since many things are better 'felt than telt') a little face with some expression on it went a long ways toward making a note more interesting (And a note in Math class went a long ways toward making Math class more interesting). I started freelancing cartoons in 1990. I've been published in *MS, Playgirl, The National Abortion Campaign Comic Book, Oh Comics* as well as these books: *Silverleaf's Choice, Women's Glibber, Kitty Libber, Sexual Harassment: Women Speak Out, Get It: A Five Minute Guide for Men Who Don't* and *Weenie-toons! Women Cartoonists Mock Cocks.*

Christine Roche resides in London and has been an active cartoonist since the early 70s. Her work has appeared in many publications including *Christine Roche: I'm not a Feminist But..., Danger! Men At Work, Pictures of Women: Sexuality,* and *New Statesman, New Society, City Limits, Feminist Review.*

Ursula Roma is a graphic designer and illustrator living in Cincinnati, Ohio. Her cartoons and illustrations have been published in *Hotwire, Bisexuality—A Reader's Guide, Feminist Bookstore News, Women's Glibber and Kitty Libber.* A brochure of her cards can be obtained by writing: Little Bear Graphics, 4236 Brookside Avenue, Cincinnati, OH 45223.

Flash Rosenberg "In a persistent, but vain, attempt to understand life (or merely to amuse friends and seduce lovers) I blurt ideas in spoken, written, sketched, sewn, photographed and filmed forms. (Or more simply I'm a humorist, performer, cartoonist, photographer and filmmaker.) My cartoons air as the radio spots *Flash Moments*, weekday mornings on the public radio station WXPN-FM in Philadelphia. *Flashpoint* cartoons have appeared in *The New York Daily News, The Village Voice, The Philadelphia Inquirer* and *The Funny Times.* My favorite color is *clear.* My favorite answer is *okay.* I am bi-Ziptual, occupying both 19107 and 10018 to do my work."

Born in 1947, near Washington, D.C., **Sharon Rudahl** has been involved in civil rights and anti-Vietnam war protests. Fine Arts graduate of the Cooper Union, New York City in 1969, Sharon began drawing underground comics as a consequence of the collapse of underground newspaper *Good Times* in San Francisco in the early 1970s, helped by friend and mentor Trina Robbins. She took a break from the struggling artist life to live in Yugoslavia with a chess grandmaster in the mid '70s. She married another chess player and moved to L.A. in 1979. She has two handsome, genius, creative sons, Jesse, born 1981, and Billy, born 1985, blond and red-haired respectively. Currently Sharon is volunteer teaching in the L.A. public schools and working as an illustrator for the Center for History in the schools at UCLA.

Mary Sativa was the first girl in her high school graduating class to stop cutting her hair (around the time Kennedy was assassinated) and wearing a bra. Nowadays she trims her bangs but otherwise remains an unreconstructed hippie. Her roman à chef *Acid Temple Ball* was published by the legendary Maurice Girodias in New York City in 1969. Subsequent work for Olympia Press, Penthouse, Playgirl. She believes sex and communism aren't really dead, merely awaiting rediscovery.

Having recently come out of an almost comatose state due to that wonderful phase of pregnancy known as the first trimester, **Theresa Henry Smith** presently finds herself still languishing in New Westminster, B.C.. With recent renewed energy she is working on her contribution to the locally produced comic book, *New!* By the time this bio is read, though, Theresa will probably, again, be in a comatose state due to being buried up to her armpits in dirty diapers and pablum spew. In the meantime, *New!* # 1 and 2 can be ordered through Tweedleying and Tweedleyang Productions/ P.O. Box 1352/Station A/ Vancouver/ British Columbia/ Canada V6C-2T2.

Noreen Stevens is a comic and activist artist living in Winnipeg, Manitoba, Canada. Her cartoon strip, *The Chosen Family,* appears in periodicals and anthologies throughout North America. As well, she is one half (with photographer Sheila Spence) of *Average Good Looks,* a terrorist girl-gang of two, which creates queer positive billboard and text images for display anywhere and everywhere. Assorted work appears in *Women's Glib* (Crossing Press) and *Weenie-toons* (Laugh Lines Press). Noreen illustrated Ellen Orleans' *Can't Keep a Straight Face* (Laugh Lines Press).

Chris Suddick is a freelance cartoonist and happily married mother of none. Her comic strips "OFF101" and "Valley Alley" have been published by *The San Jose Mercury News* since 1989.

Linda Sue Welch is a graphic illustrator. Her work—"Out Of The Darkness"—can be seen in over 2 dozen alternative/progressive newspapers and publications around the country, including *The Advocate, Equal Times, Grljock, Echo, In Step, The New Voice, Women's Glibber, Radical Chick, Holy Titty Clamps_* and others. She's currently looking for a publisher for her books *The Slicker the Hair, The More They Dare and Other Observations* and a collection of her "Out of the Darkness" panels. She uses her initials L.S. to present an androgynous, somewhat mysterious persona. She thinks diversity is very important in her work. Black, white, Asian, men, woman, children, gay, straight. When editors call to inquire about her work they are sometimes surprised to find out she's a woman sans a minority status. This pleases her greatly. For more information or comments—please contact her at P.O. Box 120793/Nashville, TN 37212.

Born in the depths of the baby boom, **Signe Wilkinson** graduated from her suburban Philadelphia high school the year the SAT scores began their slide. After acquiring a B.A. in English from a western university of middling academic reputation, Wilkinson was pathetically unprepared for real work... so became a reporter stringing for the West Chester (PA) Daily Local News. Wilkinson began drawing about the people she was supposed to be reporting on. She realized cartooning combined her interests in art and politics without taxing her interest in spelling. She began freelancing at several Philadelphia and New York publications, finally landing a fulltime job at the San Jose Mercury News in 1982. Her 3 1/2 years there were stormy but deeply instructive. Wilkinson repaid her long-suffering Mercury News editor by taking a job at the Philadelphia Daily News, where she has been drawing contentedly ever since. Wilkinson values her intensely unremarkable family life, she gardens, and every Monday night she irons her beloved husband's shirts while watching Murphy Brown.

If you enjoyed this book be sure to get Roz Warren's other books:

Women's Glib, A Collection of Women's Humor: Cartoons, stories and poems by America's funniest women wits that will knock you off your chair laughing.

Kitty Libber, Cat Cartoons by Women: Hilarious feline funnies by all the best women cartoonists.

Women's Glibber, State-of-the-Art Women's Humor: Madonna! Sex! Poultry! and much more. 310 hilarious pages.

Mothers!, Cartoons by Women: An irreverent, passionate and wickedly funny look at motherhood. For anyone who's been a mom or has a mom.

These books are available at your local bookstore or you can order directly from us. Use the coupon below, or call toll-free 800-777-1048. Please have your VISA or Mastercard ready.

roz warren is the editor of *Women's Glib: A collection of Women's Humor*, *Kitty Libber: Cat Cartoons by Women*, *Mothers! Cartoons by Women*, *Women's Glibber: State-of-the-Art Women's Humor*, *What Is This Thing Called Sex? Cartoons by Women* and *The 1994 Women's Glib Cartoon Calendar* (The Crossing Press). She's currently working on a book about women stand-up comics, and putting the finishing touches on *Women's Glib Revisited: The Ultimate Collection of Women's Humor*, both of which will be published in 1994 by The Crossing Press. Roz, a happily married radical feminist mom up in Detroit, graduated from The University of Chicago and received her law degree from Boston University Law School. She practiced law until the birth of her son. Now, an "at home" mom, she spends Quantity Time with son Tom.